partly

Wesleyan Poetry

partly

rae
armantrout

NEW AND

SELECTED POEMS,

2001–2015

Wesleyan University Press —— Middletown, Connecticut

Wesleyan University Press
Middletown CT 06459
www.wesleyan.edu/wespress
© 2016 Rae Armantrout
Manufactured in the United States of America
Designed by Mindy Basinger Hill
Typeset in Adobe Jenson Pro

Library of Congress Cataloging-in-Publication Data

Names: Armantrout, Rae, 1947–

Title: Partly : new and selected poems, 2001–2015 /
Rae Armantrout.

Description: Middletown, Connecticut :
Wesleyan University Press, [2016] |

Series: Wesleyan poetry

Identifiers: LCCN 2016001994 (print) | LCCN
2016006505 (ebook) | ISBN 9780819576552 (cloth :
alk. paper) | ISBN 9780819576569 (ebook)

Classification: LCC PS3551.R455 A6 2016 (print) |
LCC PS3551.R455 (ebook) |

DDC 811/.54—dc23

LC record available at http://lccn.loc.gov/2016001994

5 4 3 2 1

This project is supported in part by an award
from the National Endowment for the Arts.

FINALLY,

for Chuck

Contents

New Poems

Legacy

"Do words just pop
into your head?"

Some may go
unexploded.

—

"Have you thought much
about your legacy?"

I'm a legacy
prisoner.

No I'm not.

—

"What do you call precious?"

The precious doesn't
get around much

so it stays small.

Or it orbits
the same small
pronoun,

a kid
on a carousel.

"Look at me!"

It fiddles
with itself.

But I've got bigger things
to pick up

and put down.

In Front

Tree in new leaf

in front of
a brick building

with narrow
white-wood balconies

slung under panes
of glass

in which a tree

is being
dissected

before an audience
of one,

none,
hundreds.

—

New twigs
do the splits

as I once did

Exchange

City of the future
in which each subway station's stairs
lead to the ground floor
of a casino/
mall.

—

What counts
is the role
defined for each piece
by a system of rules saying
how it can move,
not the stuff
the piece is made of.

—

In the intersection,
a muscular, shirtless man
with small American
flags tied to each wrist—
so that he looks
like a wrestler—
pushes, no, shoves
then catches a stroller
piled high with plastic bags—
his stuff.

—

City of the future,
where a tramway to the top
of a peak
opens onto
a wax museum
in which
Michael Jackson
extends one gloved hand

Canary

Some folks got tortured
by folks

right afterwards
at an obscure

farmer's market
where handcrafted soda

and artisanal mining

showed
we were on the right track.

2

Canaries
served as coq-au-vin.

3

We thought of events
as landmarks

first,
then as lifebuoys,

but in this too
we were mistaken.

Mistakes

1

The subject will claim
that she has been taken
to the wrong place.

That the room
she is brought back to
is not the room she left.

That these comings and goings
are happening
to someone else,

are gathering momentum
controlled by a secret
mechanism.

That she needs to tell
someone.

2

I walk out the door
to the stone bench

without meaning to
(without meaning it?),

each step
jarring my frame

as it would anyone's

If

1

One cultivates
a garden of peculiars

"beyond reproach"

a plant like a half-
folded accordion,

a plant like a pale
rock, split in two

as if to ask,
"Where

is the original?"

2

(and a few
self-starters

with their sharp
rocket-fin leaves.)

3

You, husk-light,
forgetful,

with these
hollow bones,

this fly-away hair,

are you ready
for a new season?

If it's just this:
nutmeg-flavored latte,

"pumpkin"

Surplus

I sat on the patio and wrote

Each afternoon I would sit on the patio where one waggish, unmoored
tendril nodded emphatically and the tree cast a web of nervous yet
resilient shadows, while the crickets had no idea what they were
insisting on —

but then what's an idea?

I might visualize living sculpture (in which subjectivity, unable
to either detach itself from the body or direct it, had a public
experience of itself as surplus) without wishing to harm anyone.

In fact, I did.

Assembly

1

With large red lips,
a ceramic fish face
in a pink knit pouch
from which spinelike
sticks protrude
is suspended
above the work station.

2

Though ghosts don't exist,
electrons on the mirror's surface
absorb arriving photons and,
in their excitement,
emit others that
come back your way,
replicate a woman.

Outburst

1

What do you like best
about the present?

Reflection—

its spangle
and its non-
locality:

those eucalyptus leaves
as points of light

splashed
over this windshield.

2

What if every moment
is a best guess
on a pop quiz?

As if waking up,
I stop explaining

Tony Soprano's outburst

to his aggravated
henchmen.

Taking Place

Once we liked the conspicuous
but constrained,

the push-up bra
under the shirtwaist,

a small bow
at the throat,

the appearance
of a struggle

toward the diminutive,
the punctum.

—

The slender
second hand

jerking forward
as if helpless,

making its same sound.

—

We might stand
in a thicket

where a battle had
taken place

and be thrilled
by the far-off roar

of traffic

Easily

The models
in the Gentlemen's Club ad
are posed
with pink mouths slack,
eyes narrowed
to slits.

Show me stunned resentment—

the way
the world absorbs
an insult
it won't easily
forget

Partly

In this ad
for Newfoundland,
an old woman
steps onto the porch
of the lone house
on a remote cove
and shakes a white sheet
at a partly cloudy sky

as if

—

Matched burgundy berries
on adjacent stems,

perfect ear bobs,

with no one
wearing them

Parallel Worlds Theory

When a new bar called
The Air-Conditioned Lounge
opens and its sign
is in old-time cursive
this is ironic because

the building
is a concrete box
and the sign
looks like a gift card,
no,

this is ironic
because its claim
is true
but does nothing
to distinguish it.

Either this sign
is a reversal
of the many
novel yet dubious
claims we endure

or it expresses
guarded nostalgia
for a time
when it was that easy
to be cool.

Those branches
are good

because they remind me
of others.

The others
are the same

but small

Word Problems

If a fat man
with one earlobe distended
by a large ring

and a thin man
in a heavy neck chain

sit together
checking email

    The real is made up
    of things minus
    appearance

near eucalyptus strands
of green crescents

and their shadows—flighty
half-moons

    while the soul
    is made up
    of appearance
    minus things

Action Potential

Who sequesters
negatively charged
ions
and waits.

—

Milton's devils
make me sad—

the way
Satan must cross
chaos and dark night
hour by hour
to reach us,
actually flying
as if space were real,
the way he stops
and asks directions

—

Who runs
along the tops
of trains, leaping
from car to car,
ratcheted
into the present
in his topcoat

if there is no

Torn

1

If the whole ragged
current
were a creature,

we could expect it
to both anticipate
and remember

the splash it makes
here
on this rock,

its acrobatic performance
of momentum

run through

to the point of
distraction.

In this series,
sleeper agents

live our lives—
some version of our lives—

with (what might be)
this difference:

most of what they do
is feigned,

but not all.

That's what keeps us
riveted.

Divisor

1

How pairs
of power lines

hold gray
interstates

between them

2

List of ways
the body
befriends the body:

strumming
the left toes
over the right
as if;

causing each finger
to touch its mate
and press.

It's a good thing
the body's
split.

The two sides
can make up

while the head
goes on

saying what it's like

Life's Work

I

Did I say I was a creature
of habit?

I meant the opposite.

I meant behavior
is a pile of clothes

I might or might not wear.

Before all the sowing and reaping
could go on for centuries,

before the calendar,
I must have been convinced

that my movements
were both mandated

and blessed.

2

I've never been an old woman
knitting by a fire,

but I've played one
in images

where it meant being foolish
or wise, a mistress

of distraction's
indirection.

To rock while entwining
is life's work,

but I am reckless,
restless

The Difficulty

This film, like many others,
claims we'll enjoy life
now that we've come through

difficulties, dangers
so incredibly condensed
that they must be over.

If the hardship
was undergone by others,
we identified with them

and, if the danger was survived
by simpler life forms,
they're included in this moment

when the credits roll
and we don't know
when to stand

The Ether

We're out
past the end

game where things
get fuzzy,

less thingy,

though in past times
we practiced

precision
concrete as a slot machine.

But to be precise
you need to stop

a moment
which turns out to be

impracticable
and besides

speed is of the essence.

Don't worry.

"Of" can take care
of itself

and it's fine
to say "essence"

now that it's understood
to mean ether,

a kind of filler
made either

of inattention
or absorption

somewhere near
the Planck length

What We Can Say

1

"The traumatized rats practiced excessive self-grooming."

Thinking is practice.

The idea that we can improve
is a form of self-grooming.

Adjusting to the rapidly changing orientations
of figures on a screen
can feel like having a succession of ideas,
each of which must be incorporated
into our current attitude.

To incorporate change without disorientation
is to win.

2

"Ideas link things in novel ways."

We might say that music
attempts to make time
into space—visualizable, repeatable.

(We may have said this previously.)

Or we may say music
attempts to make space into time
so that between the current
stances of the musicians
there exists something like flow.

But there is really no direction
in comparison,
only the desire
that two entities
become one,

as if reduction in number
were the purpose
of all thought.

3

Though it's also true
that one gets bored.

Voices

You're boring, people.

America doesn't want
to watch you sleep.

America doesn't want to hear you
think about tacos.

—

Men in uniforms
are clubbing onlookers.

I've been informed
this is all for show.

These are not real
audience members.

Overhead

Sleep is insistent
voices, mine

or anyone's,
running

some scam.

Peace is empty
palaces

adrift
overhead.

"How you create
this level

of experience
So

from a recording
standpoint

Altered Cage

1

Don't have time for jogging?

to buy wool and lumber

always had some testimony

altered cage

But tell me sir

2

Forty years' experience
with turning experience

into topiary
makes me

a real insider.

3

The way whatever
Midas touched

turned gold,
whatever I recognize

is mine.
I'd like to leave

some of "mine"
with you,

but it's one thing
that can't be
shared.

Transport

1

Would you like the world
to end now

(in your lifetime)

so you don't miss
anything?

Would you like the world
to go on

so that someone
later

might feel as
you once did?

Did you feel anxious
when alone?

Did you feel restless
at parties?

2

If clear yellow petals
are enough

like sails,
I'll be well

away.

I'll be on my way
to this

late summer dusk

Sockets

You feed yourself
frothy maple Greek

mousse whip. Each
bite a virgin.

Promiscuity and sloth
no longer sins

after what you've done.

———

Or you have perfect
understanding

of past events
which no longer

seem unjust.
Your "O"

a sphere,
a song.

———

But
in the afterlife,

roots rip
from your sockets,

new brains
in their tips,

scouting for water

Particular

1

Rough, squat, bent,
crabbed, cranky.

A crank is a person
who is over-enthusiastic
about a particular topic.

To be particular
is to be choosy.

A particle
is a body

whose extent
and internal structure,
if any,

are irrelevant.

2

You there,

let's dispense with
these "properties"

of matter—

such anachronistic clothes
as ghosts wear.

Let's be mirrors
facing mirrors,

fall
in love

Lie

I lay down
the acidification
of the ocean
with a sly smile.

Unstoppable
beats fiery impact
every time.

~~~~

But the sweet yellow
shoulders of the road—

the up and up
into same blossom.

I'd like to hold these
in reserve.

2

"Protect your identity"
says Mileage.com
three times today
as if it knew something.

I may want to fly cheap,
cruise in luxury,
buy a walk-in tub
and burial insurance.

—

I may want to lie still
and think about my choices.

Before

I

Would my life be like
a letter to you then?

We never wrote letters.

⁓

I'm passing the signs
we slipped by together.

There goes Soda and Swine.

That name is funny
because it's a joke we shared
about alliteration,
right?

⁓

If I can describe
the feeling
of your absence
precisely, which means
using the names
of things

⁓

Buds blacken
against blanched light

as ever

St. Didacus' bells'
ditty

reminds us
of itself,

something old and
automated,

dividing before
from now

again and again,
these two

for a moment
still similar

Followers

1

This blank sky

between parallel wires

reserved

for penmanship

practice.

2

The cold rays
of the bristle cone,

she writes—

she who admires
imitations.

Such sparse coronas
surrounding

every knobby
fist!

"Naught"

must follow

"for"

which will come

after "all."

Come as "always,"

walking backwards

Song

If shadows slide down
a cliff face
slowly—
not falling—
but softening
its colors,
I'll wait.

—

Or if shadows
bend and straighten,
repeatedly, and
the intervals between
are not fixed

—

If the sun
clears the wall behind me
and the little table
brightens

—

If the background is still
while the foreground is in motion—
or if it's the other way,
I'll wait

Approximate

Wait, I haven't found
the right word yet.

Poem means
homeostasis.

"Is as"

As is

Film is enough
like death.

In a bright light
at the far end,
attractive strangers gesture.

They are searching
the system
for systemic threats.

I was going
to pay attention.

Attention passes
through a long cord

into the past
progressive

FROM *Up to Speed*

Up to Speed

Streamline to instantaneous
voucher in/voucher out
system.

The plot winnows.

The Sphinx
wants me to guess.

Does a road
run its whole length
at once?

Does a creature
curve to meet
itself?

Whirlette!

———

Covered or cupboard
breast? Real

housekeeping's
kinesthesiac. Cans

held high
to counterbalance "won't."

Is it
such agendas

which survive
as souls?

—

Vagueness is personal!

A wall of concrete bricks,
right here,
while sun surveys its grooves

and I try "instantly"
then "forever."

But the word is
way back,
show-boating.

Light is "with God"

(light, the traveler).

—

Are you the come-on
and the egress?

One who hobbles by
determinedly?

Not yet?

Form

Dear April, I appreciated the way the paragraphs were all about the same
length. I especially liked how your sentences appeared
to relate to one another. It was getting late,
they said. Solemn,
blunt flash of sun
off the window
of a Coors Light
truck.

On a fence across the street, wings of a wooden chicken
spun backward. Everyone
had reason to be proud.
I could handle symbols
without being manipulated by them.
Like a stone butch, you might say, but that's
only connotation.

Meanwhile, in the photographs,
my expression was fading,
as if my darling,
Ambiguity,
were just another word
for death

What is the nature of the resting state
but gaseous longing/
regret?
In the original/
final form—

without objects

Currency

I stare at the edge

until the word
tulip

comes up
where I thought it might.

But the lag-time
is a problem.

The swollen, yellow
head of Tweety-Bird

now offered
at the border

as balloon
or ceramic,

as baby
plus crucifixion,

as distended
incredulity

held toward the cars,
as silence

The Fit

In a fit of repugnance
each moment
rips itself in half,

producing a twin.

—

In a coming-of-age story
each dream
produces me:

an ignorance
on the point of revelation.

—

I'm at a side table

in a saloon
in Alaska,

my eye on the door
where a flood of strangers
pours in.

—

The door or the window?

It's morning.

Middle Men

The story is told from the view-point of two young technicians, one fat and one thin, who must give their superior a moment by moment account of their attempts to monitor the subject. Suspense occurs, occasionally, when they must tell the superior that they're having trouble keeping the listening devices within range. We sympathize with the hunted subject, but also with the clearly competent, frequently exasperated technicians, whose situation is, after all, much more like our own.

End Times

I

Galaxies run from us. "Don't look!"
Was this the meaning
of the warning in the Garden?
When a dreamer sees she's dreaming,
it causes figments to disperse.

2

Black bars and dots
of low cloud,

almost a signature,
reflected on a sunset marsh.

Luxuriant and spurious code

as art,
as if we were meant to think,

"Beautiful!" —
so we do

and a ripple
travels in one spot.

When something reaches
the speed of light

it will appear to freeze,

growing gradually
less meaningful.

3

Being able to look at water soothes the anxious emptiness between thoughts. I think again and again about the way the water looks. I can keep each thought longer by writing it down. The process of writing this sentence is time-consuming in itself, almost irritatingly slow—so now I rush and jumble the letters. It occurs to me that later I may not be able to read what I wrote.

Seconds

1

The point is to see through
the dying,

who pinch non-existent
objects from the air

sequentially,

to this season's
laying on of
withered leaves?

2

A moment is everything

one person

(see below)

takes in simultaneously

though some

or much of what

a creature feels

may not reach

conscious awareness

and only a small part

(or none) of this

will be carried forward

to the next instant.

3

Any one
not seconded

burns up in rage.

Next Generations

1

But, on "Star Trek," we *aren't* the Borg,

the aggressive conglomerate,

each member part humanoid, part

machine, bent on assimilating

foreign cultures. In fact,

we destroy their ship,

night after night,

in preparation for sleep.

2

We sense something's wrong

when our ideal selves

look like contract players.

The captain plays what's left

of believable authority

as a Shakespearean actor.

The rest are there to show surprise

each time

the invading cube appears—

until any response seems stupid.

But we forgive them.

We've made camp

in the glitch

Upper World

If sadness
is akin to patience,

we're back!

Pattern recognition
was our first response

to loneliness.

Here and there were *like*
one place.

But we need to triangulate,
find someone to show.

——

There's a jolt, quasi-electric,
when one of our myths
reverts to abstraction.

Now we all know
every name's Eurydice,
briefly returned
from blankness

and the way back
won't bear scrutiny.

High voices
over rapid-pulsing synthesizers
intone, "without you" —

which is soothing.

We prefer meta-significance:

the way the clouds exchange
white scraps
in glory.

No more wishes.

No more bungalows
behind car-washes
painted the color of
swimming pools

Once

Once there were people among whom
each one had to be convinced
she was the most wondrous alive
in order to go on living.
It was creation ex nihilo
all over again.
Crews were organized in shifts.
"Skin as white as snow
and hair as black as night," they chanted.
In off hours, everyone smirked
at the result
and called it sentimental.

2

At last the camp melodrama
of Dan Rather

relaxes

into the pseudo
sibling raillery
of the local newscast.

Since we're being escorted
from moment to moment

by what's already
familial,

we should be able
to follow this track
back
home
to our previous thought.

3

The opposite
of nothingness

is direction

This Time

1

It seemed normal.

Just last minute's
hard scrabble of brush
                    left out—

and now laced
with rollicking flickers.

What?

With unwound cassette tape.

Or tape wound
stick to stick
to send the last signal.

2

Dreams write themselves.

The sense of being addressed
lasts minutes.

The milkweed weaves itself
an empty cotton dress. Then

a tiny woman
comes out at the top.

She brings the people
their first map

in the form of a spider's web.

This time
no one is suspicious.

Imaginary Places

Reading, we are allowed to follow someone else's train of thought as it starts off for an imaginary place. This train has been produced for us—or rather materialized and extended until it is almost nothing like the ephemeral realizations with which we're familiar. To see words pulled one by one into existence is to intrude on a privacy of sorts. But we *are* familiar with the contract between spectator and performer. Now the text isn't a train but an actress/model who takes off her school uniform piece by piece alone with the cameraman. She's a good girl playing at being bad, all the time knowing better. She invites us to join her in that knowledge. But this is getting us nowhere.

Almost

1

Almost all the words we've said to one another are gone
and if they were retrieved, verbatim, we might not acknowledge
them.
But the *tenor* of our talk
has been constant across decades!
(Tenor is what we meant by "soul.")

For instance,
the way we joke
by using non-sequiturs, elliptical remarks
which deliberately suppress context
in advance
of time's rub-out.

2

"When size really counts,"
the billboard says

showing the product
tiny,

in one corner,

so we need to search for it.
Come find me.

I stand
behind these words.

FROM *Next Life*

Tease

For lack of which
we put ourselves
in a cop's place

as he puts himself
inside the head
of a serial killer rapist

who appears to be
teasing the police.

—

Bare tree
is to human skeleton

as the holy spirit
likens objects

briefly

to make the world up
of provisional pairs.

—

It makes sense
to turn that corner
in a black sedan

and to write down
everything that passes.

To quick-step up the street
in a knit red cap
one time only.

———

Red cap is to
one time only
as

Two, Three

Sad, fat boy in pirate hat.
Long, old, dented,
copper-colored Ford.

How many traits
must a thing have
in order to be singular?

(Echo persuades us
everything we say
has been said at least once
                before.)

Two plump, bald men
in gray tee-shirts
and tan shorts

are walking a small bulldog—
followed by the eyes
of an invisible third person.

The Trinity was born
from what we know
of the bitter

symbiosis of couples.
Can we reduce echo's sadness
by synchronizing our speeches?

Is it the beginning or end
of *real* love
when we pity a person

because, in him,
we see ourselves?

Close

1

As if a single scream
gave birth

to whole families
of traits

such as "flavor," "color,"
"spin"

and this tendency to cling.

2

Dry, white frazzle
in a blue vase—

beautiful

a frozen swarm
of incommensurate wishes.

3

Slow, blue, stiff
are forms

of crowd behavior,

mass hysteria.

Come close.

The crowd is made of
little gods

and there is still
no heaven

Thing

We love our cat
for her self
regard is assiduous
and bland,

for she sits in the small
patch of sun on our rug
and licks her claws
from all angles

and it is far
superior
to "balanced reporting"

though, of course,
it is also
the very same thing.

Empty

The present
must be kept empty
so that anything
can happen:

    The Queen of England visits
    Amanda's hot tub

    as a prophylaxis?

a discrepancy
between one's view of things
and what comes to pass.

—

It's ironic when something
has a meaning to someone

    "Gotta go
    Gotta go
    Gotta go
    right now"

other than that
intended by the speaker.

    sings the bladder-control model
    from the fidgety TV
    above the dying woman's bed.

—

It's ironic when a set
contains no elements.

Of a person, frivolous.
Of a body, shrunken.

The Subject

It's as if we've just been turned human
in order to learn
that the beetle we've caught
and are now devouring
is our elder brother
and that we
are a young prince.

—

I was just going to click
on "Phoebe is changed
into a mermaid
tomorrow!" when suddenly
it all changed
into the image
of a Citizen watch.

—

If each moment is in love
with its image
in the mirror of
adjacent moments

(as if matter stuttered),

then, of course, we're restless!

"What is a surface?"
we ask,

trying to change the subject.

Reversible

1

Try this.

Shadows of leaves
between shadows of venetian blinds

bounce

like holes

across the scroll of a
player-piano.

But are similes reversible?

Try this.

Trunk of a palm tree
as the leg

of a one-legged
ballerina.

2

That's a bad
Sean Connery, but
a good Prince.

We wake up to an empty room
addressing itself in scare quotes.

"Happen" and "now"
have been smuggled out,

to arrive safely in the past tense.

We come home to a cat
made entirely of fish.

Yonder

1

Anything cancels
everything out.

If each point
is a singularity,

thrusting all else
aside for good,

"good" takes the form
of a throng
of empty chairs.

Or it's ants
swarming a bone.

2

I'm afraid
I don't love
my mother
who's dead

though I once—
what does "once" mean?—
did love her.

So who'll meet me over yonder?
I don't recognize the place names.

Or I do, but they come
from televised wars.

Framing

FOR ROBERT CREELEY

What you won't see today:

juniper's tough skein.

—

The rolling
hummocks

have grown syntax—

tassels and bells—

for careless
wings to be among.

—

The tic
in articulation.

—

The present is cupped

by a small effort
of focus—

its muscular surround.

You're left out.

Make It New

Shaking the parts of speech
like fluff
in a snow globe—

the way sleep scrambles
life's detritus.

Each poem says,
"I'm desperate"

then, "Everything
must go!"

(To hear something familiar here
leads to careful laughter.)

"Go" where?

The steady pressure
on the accelerator
can be stipulated
in advance

as can the stubby bushes
blurred in peripheral vision.

And someone will have set down
a diner or a gas station
at a desolate crossroads

and tried naming it
to evoke
the whole human situation

while
satirizing
the impulse to do so.

What that name will be
is the one thing we don't know

Again

General Foods ads from the '50s line a restaurant's walls.
It's not nostalgic; nostalgia requires a place
to which we might want to go back.

It's our felt distance
from the supposed past
as collectible,

our credulities and
incredulities
as collectibles.

The sketchier the better, the way
a simply drawn young mother

pours milk from a pitcher
onto Corn Flakes

for a Cool Start

and the compressed
airiness
of Rice Krispies.

2

The static seems jumpy tonight,
anxious, randomized, but

perhaps not truly random.

That's what worries some of us.

Hollywood itself

tells us the background
is composed of voices

speaking from beyond
their own annihilation.

We ought to be frightened
of the reconstituted

pronominal fizz
that invades us,

the wavery, weasely persistence

which, once we start to listen,
demands to be heard

Yoohoo

Sun lights up a pelt
of dust on the receiver.

Being unexpected,
this is a kind of call.

Cross names out
and things are all made up

of contrary, percussive,
adjectival tugs.

I remember someone
wrestled an angel,

                a signal.

The present's chronic
revision

which a poem
reenacts.

The open vowel
(peek-a-boo)
pelvis

through which you
"came into this world"

sits on the shelf

in a mausoleum
now,

world on either side of it

Next Life

Last of all and
most reluctantly
you said goodbye to
"near"
and "far away."

Fuzzy-minded
clouds sprout

from one another's
foreheads.

But you were more exact.

You unzipped yourself
in the dark

back there,

counted yourself
in half

and cut.

That was before numbers.

3

"Don't be a commodity;
be a concept:"

a ghostly configuration
of points or parts—

trivia snippets—

which appears inside
locked cabinets.

Be untraceable
but easy to replicate.

Be relative.

Be twice as far
and halfway back

Twizzle

He who finds a knot
in himself
where a soft expanse should be

will want to tell
the nearest person to him.

But this can be known
now

and lived later on

so the start of it
is always somewhere else.

—

Evenly hovering attention:
pocked concrete.

Long tangles of gray-
green eucalyptus leaves

twizzle,
throwing sharp shadows.

If I could just signal
so variously.

—

The trees upstart.

By "virgin"
we meant inaccessible
just now,

and by "inaccessible"
we meant original.

The virgin birth
can only happen once

everywhere

and doesn't dare stop

FROM *Versed*

Results

1

Click here to vote
on who's ripe
for a makeover

or takeover

in this series pilot.

Votes are registered
at the server
and sent back

as results.

2

Click here to transform

oxidation
into digestion.

From this point on,
it's a lattice
of ends
disguised as means:

the strangler fig,

the anteater.

3

I've developed the ability
to revise
what I'm waiting for

so that letter
becomes dinner
gradually

while the contrapuntal
nodding
of the Chinese elm leaves

redistributes
ennui

Versed

The self-monitoring function
of each cell
"writ large,"

personified—
a person.

⁓

The "Issues of the Day"
are mulled steadily
by surrogates.

⁓

Metaphor forms
a crust
beneath which
the crevasse
of each experience.

⁓

Traversed
by robotic surveyors.

⁓

Mother yells, "Good job!"
when he drops the stick,

"Good job!"
when he walks in her direction

Address

The way my interest
in their imaginary
kiss

is secretly addressed
to you.

—

Without intention

prongs of ivy
mount the posts
supporting the freeway.

It would be possible to say
each leaf

circumscribes hope

or that each leaf,
fastidiously coming
to one point,

suggests a fear
of the unknown.

—

These glossy,
laced-up, high-heel boots

(each leaf)

addressed to you

Vehicles

Pairing matched fragments,
then pausing—

archly?—

Mozart creates a universe
out of pleasantries.

"How is everything
for you today?"

the hostess
at the front desk asks.

—

If *that* (head-on car-crash)
had happened, we say,

all this
would not have been—

like "having been"
were a lasting thing:

the small tree
on the highway meridian

having been lit up
for a moment now

by sun breaking through cloud

—

Look how
we "attempted to express ourselves."

Every one of these words is wrong.

It wasn't us.
Or we made no real attempt.
Or there is no discernible difference
between self and expression.

———

What was meant by "streamlining"
we might guess,

but what was meant by streamlining
as value added
to this

already bulky,
even bulbous,

baby-pink conveyance,

we can only ask

A Resemblance

As a word is
mostly connotation,

matter is mostly
aura?

Halo?

(The same loneliness
that separates me

from what I call
"the world.")

—

Quiet, ragged
skirt of dust

encircling a ceramic
gourd.

—

Look-alikes.

"Are you happy now?"

—

Would I like
a vicarious happiness?

Yes!

Though I suspect
yours of being defective,

forced

Operations

This child fights cancer
with the help
of her celebrity fan club,

says,
"Now I know how hard it is
to be a movie star."

—

"Hey,
my avatar's not working!"

—

This small hawk on a wire
above tangled flowers.

—

Speech, too, was thought
to be inhabited
by a god.

Then hunger
invented light.

Guess

1

The jacaranda, for instance, is beautiful
but not serious.

That much
I can guess.

And that the view
is softened by curtains.

That the present moment
is an exception,

is the queen bee
a hive serves,

or else an orphan.

2

So the jacaranda
is foreign and extravagant.

It gestures in the distance.

Between there and here
you ask

what game
we should play next week.

So we'll be alive
next week,

continuing
what you may or may not

mean to be
an impossible flirtation

Scumble

What if I were turned on by seemingly innocent words
such as "scumble," "pinky," or "extrapolate?"

What if I maneuvered conversation in the hope that
others would pronounce these words?

Perhaps the excitement would come from the way the
other person touched them lightly and carelessly with
his tongue.

What if "of" were such a hot button?

"Scumble of bushes."

What if there were a hidden pleasure
in calling one thing
by another's name?

Presto

"Breaking
Anna Nicole news

as she buries
her son."

—

"What do you want
to be?"

Skeleton suits
and Superman outfits—

inappropriate touching
on drugstore racks.

—

Presto!

Pairs of flies
re-tie

the old knot
mid-air.

—

Blonde wigs and
wizard caps.

"I want to go back!"

Invisible knot.

I want to be that!

What We Mean

Oh Princess,
you apple-core afloat

in coke
in a Styrofoam cup,
on an end-table,

you dust, glass, book, crock, thorn, moon.

Oh Beauty who fell asleep
on your birthday,

we swipe at you.

—

How are we defining "dream?"

An exaggerated sense

of the relevance
of these details,

of "facts"
as presented?

A peculiar
reluctance to ask

presented by whom
and in what space?

—

By space we mean
the collapsible

whirligig
of attention,

the figuring and
reconfiguring

of charges

among orbits
      (obits)
that has taken forever

Later

1

To be beautiful
and powerful enough
for someone
to want to break me
                    up

into syndicated ripples.

Later I'll try
to rise from these dead.

2

How much would this body
have had to be otherwise in order
not to be mine,

for this world
not to exist?

When would that difference
have had to begin?

3

The old lady invited me to her soirée. Maybe I was even older than she
was. I was mysterious, at any rate, a rarity, until the room filled up. Then
not. When she handed out chocolates, she forgot me. I gesticulated as if it
were funny and she gave me two pink creams. Me! As if I would have ever
wanted these!

4

They drive me
out to sea.

Secretly, I am still
_____, the mysterious.

I speak in splashes.

Later
I have the lonely dream

Own

Woman in a room near mine moans, "I'm dying. I want
to be fine. It's my body!
Don't let me! Don't touch me!"

—

By definition,
I'm the blip
floating across my own
"field of vision . ."

—

On closed eyes I see the spartan wall of the ICU
covered in a scrambled hodge-podge of sticky notes,
crossing one another at all angles,
illegibly written over, snippets of reference,
madly irrelevant.

—

Symbolism as the party face of paranoia.

Chorus of expert voices beyond my door, forever
dissecting my case.

"But the part is sick
of representing the whole."

—

"We will prevail,"
says the leader on multiple
screens. The words
are empty, but he's there
inside the lie
everyone believes—
that nothing
will really change. He's become pure
being, insisting
only on insistence.

—

A crowd (scene) of cells, growing wildly,
by random access to stock types,
(Play any role you like and go on
forever. Who is speaking?)
Able to draw blood vessels to itself
by emitting a mock distress call.

—

From deep time,
patterns
on my grandmother's crockery
rise
to cover my closed eyelids,
lumpy fruits and flowers, brown
against a cream background.

—

Dream that Aaron is telling friends to be quiet because he's listening to a
rumble, a white noise voice from his own intestines which he believes is
telling him how to save me. "SHH!" he says to anyone who speaks.

On Your Way

On your way to The Sea of Reeds you will meet the Soul Devouring
Demon. You've heard it all before and you believe it. Why not?
Why would they lie? You must wear the beetle amulet to avoid being
consumed. But it's also true that you can't really know until it's actually
happening. So you have a sort of knowledge which, even if later
confirmed in each detail, is still not real knowledge. He will weigh your
heart and, if it's too heavy, you'll be swallowed up. What is this extra
element that is mingled in when you arrive at the ordained spot?

Around

Time is pleased
to draw itself
        out,
permit itself
pendulous loops,

to allow them
meaning,

this meaning,

as it goes

    along.

     —

Chuck and I are pleased
to have found a spot
where my ashes can be scattered.
It looks like a construction site
now
but it's adjacent
to a breathtaking, rocky coast.
Chuck sees places
where he might snorkel.
We're being shown through
by a sort of realtor.
We're interested but can't get her
to fix the price.

     —

"The future
is all around us."

It's a place,

anyplace
where we don't exist.

Dark Matter

Who am I
to experience a burst
of star formation?

I know this —

after the first rush
of enthusiasm

any idea
recedes and dims.

2

Each one
is the inverse
shape of what's
missing.

3

One might try
summing
the matter up

in a single
Judas kiss,

all bitter-sweet
complicity

and feigned ignorance

Unbidden

The ghosts swarm.
They speak as one
person. Each
loves you. Each
has left something
undone.

—

Did the palo verde
blush yellow
all at once?

Today's edges
are so sharp

they might cut
anything that moved.

—

The way a lost
word

will come back
unbidden.

You're not interested
in it now,

only
in knowing
where it's been.

Simple

FOR AARON KORKEGIAN

Complex systems can arise
from simple rules.

It's not
that we *want* to survive,
it's that we've been drugged
and made to act
as if we do

while all the while
the sea breaks
and rolls, painlessly, under.

If we're not copying it,
we're lonely.

Is this the knowledge
that demands to be
passed down?

Time is made from swatches
of heaven and hell.

If we're not killing it,
we're hungry.

Djinn

Haunted, they say, believing
the soft, shifty
dunes are made up
of false promises.

Many believe
whatever happens
is the other half
of a conversation.

Many whisper
white lies
to the dead.

"The boys are doing really well."

Some think
nothing is so
until it has been witnessed.

They believe
the bits are iffy;

the forces that bind them,
absolute.

Missing Persons

God and Mother
went the same way.

—

What's a person to us
but a contortion
of pressure ridges
palpable
long after she is gone?

—

A thin old man in blue jeans,
back arched, grimaces
at the freezer compartment.

—

Lying in the tub,
I'm telling them—

the missing persons—

that a discrepancy
is a pea

and I am a Princess.

Integer

1

One what?

One grasp?

No hands.

No collection

of stars. Something dark

pervades it.

2

Metaphor
is ritual sacrifice.

It kills the look-alike.

No,
metaphor is homeopathy.

A healthy cell
exhibits contact inhibition.

3

These temporary credits
will no longer be reflected
in your next billing period.

4

"Dark" meaning
not reflecting,

not amenable
to suggestion.

Hoop

God twirled
across the face of
what cannot be named
since it was not moving.

God was momentum then,
that impatience
with interruption,

stamping time's blanks
with its own image.

Now her theme will be
that she has escaped
certain destruction,

that she is
impossibly lucky.

This theme should be jaunty
but slightly discordant,

coming in, as it does,
so late.

The character
associated with this theme
should be dressed
in markedly old-fashioned clothing—

a hoop skirt perhaps—

while everyone else
is in cut-offs,

ready for the barbeque.

Remaining

1

It might be 1976. "Hotel California" is on every sound system. It tells us we're jaded—which is oddly terrific. This isn't going to take long at all. "Been there, done that," we will soon say. Tried to find the door. Futility features a soaring solo.

2

My parents are calling. "I Love Lucy" is about to start. It's funny the way Lucy wants to go too, do what Desi does. She wheedles and schemes. Her efforts, however, are not as impressive as Wile. E. Coyote's. When he fails, human ingenuity is foiled. Now Lucy is getting a laugh. She and Little Ricky can't open the door.

Anchor

"Widely expected,
if you will,
cataclysm."

Things I'd say,
am saying,

to persons no longer
present.

Yards away trim junipers
make their customary
bows.

"Oh, no thank you"
to any of it.

If you watch me
from increasing distance,

I am writing this
always

Pass

Single cells

become like-minded,

forming a consensus

or quorum.

Bioluminescence and virulence

are two ways

we describe the feeling

they share then.

With effort,

humans can approach

this condition.

"Synchronized swimming

has afforded me

a wonderful life,"

says one informant.

Why not?

I too would like

to exert power

over time,

to pass it,

aggressively, dramatically,

and forget all about it

until even

the meaning of the word

"pass"

gets lost

in a rosy glow.

FROM *Money Shot*

Staging

1

Everything will be made new.

The precision coupling
and uncoupling,

the studied
blocking
and folding

have already begun.

2

Stillness of gauzy curtains

and the sound
of distant vacuums.

Prolonged sigh
of traffic

and the downward
curve of fronds.

The spray
of all possible paths.

Define possible.

Across

1

Wood
under an oval lake
of glass

across which
this morning
parallel wakes
appear,

gleaming bits
of skin, akin
to happiness?

2

Of course, "across"
is metaphorical.

But light is violent and weightless.

Light is the wail of atoms
pressed to touch.

It is reluctance

raised
to absolute velocity

Prayers

1

We pray
and the resurrection happens.

Here are the young
again,

sniping and giggling,

tingly
as ringing phones.

2

All we ask
is that our thinking

sustain momentum,
identify targets.

The pressure
in my lower back
rising to be recognized
as pain.

The blue triangles
on the rug
repeating.

Coming up,
a discussion
on the uses
of torture.

The fear
that all *this*
will end.

The fear
that it won't.

Fuel

The sun on my back
like your hand

at night,
in bed,

and then again,

your hand
on my back at night

like the sun
has burned through

two-thirds of its fuel.

2

That you adorn the fallen.

That your heads
and shafts
are smooth,

cool,
a spongy marble.

That you are stock-still
and spontaneous at once.

That you *are* one

(as we always thought
we knew).

The Gift

You confuse
the image of a fungus

with the image of a dick
in my poem

(understandably)

and three days later
a strange toadstool

(white shaft, black cap,
five inches tall)

appears
between the flagstones
in our path.

We note
the invisible

web
between fence posts

in which dry leaves
are gently rocked.

Spin

That we are composed
of dimensionless points

which nonetheless spin,

which nonetheless exist
in space,

which is a mapping
of dimensions.

—

The pundit says
the candidate's speech
hit
"all the right points,"

hit "fed-up" but "not bitter,"
hit "not hearkening back."

—

Light strikes our eyes
and we say, "Look *there!*"

Bubble Wrap

"Want to turn on CNN,
see if there've been any
disasters?"

—

In the dream,
you slip inside me.

Ponzi scheme; rhyme scheme.

The child wants his mother
to put her head
where his is, see
what he sees.

—

In the dream
inside the dream,

our new roommates
are arguing:

"These are not
Astroturf calls,

and we're all populists
now."

—

Now an engine's
single indrawn breath.

(The black hole
at the heart

of it
is taking it

all back.)

⸺

An immigrant
sells scorpions
of twisted electrical wire
in front of the Rite Aid.

Answer

a moment of stillness,
demanding an answer.

When does a moment end?

—

Starbucks prayer,
"Make morning good again."

—

Leaf shadows on pavement:

word meaning to slide
carelessly,
repeatedly,
to absentmindedly caress.

—

For I so loved the world

that I set up
my only son to

be arrested.

Autobiography: Urn Burial

I could say
"authenticity"

will have been about trying
to overtake the past,

inhabit it
long enough to look around,

say "Oh,"

but the past is tricky,

holds off.

So are we really moving?

Or is this something
like the way

form appears
to chase function?

I might hazard that my life's course
has been somewhat unusual.
When I say that, I hear both
an eager claim
and a sentence that attempts to distance itself
by adopting the style
of a 19th-century English gentleman.
The failed authority
of such sentences is soothing,
like watching Masterpiece Theatre.

When I recount my experiences,
whatever they may have been,
I'm aware of piping tunes
I've heard before.
Or jumbled snatches of familiar tunes.
The fancy cannot cheat
for very long, can it?
In the moment of experience,
one may drown
while another looks on.

Soft Money

They're sexy
because they're needy,
which degrades them.

They're sexy because
they don't need you.

They're sexy because they pretend
not to need you,

but they're lying,
which degrades them.

They're beneath you
and it's hot.

They're across the border,
rhymes with dancer —

they don't need
to understand.

They're content to be
(not *mean*),

which degrades them
and is sweet.

They want to be
the thing-in-itself

and the thing-for-you —

Miss Thing—

but can't.

They want to be you,
but can't,

which is so hot.

Advent

In front of the craft shop,
a small nativity,
mother, baby, sheep
made of white
and blue balloons.

—

Sky
      god
            girl.

Pick out the one
that doesn't belong.

—

Something

close to nothing
           flat
from which,

fatherless,
everything has come.

With

It's well
that things should stir
inconsequentially
around me
like this
patina of shadow,
flicker, whisper,
so that
I can be still.

———

I write things down
to show others
later
or to show myself
that I am not alone with
my experience.

———

"With"
is the word that
comes to mind,
but it's not
the right word here.

Outage

1

We like to think
that the mind
controls the body.

We send the body on a mission.

We don't feel the body,
but we receive conflicting reports.

The body is catching flak
or flies.

The body is sprouting grapefruit.

The body is under-
performing in heavy
trading.

2

Reception is spotty.

Someone "just like me"
is born
in the future
and I don't feel a thing?

Like only goes so far.

Duration

Those flurries
of small pecks

my mother called
leaky faucet kisses.

Late sun winks
from a power line

beyond the neighbor's tree.
In heaven,

where repetition's
not boring—

Silver whistles
of blackbirds

needle
the daylong day.

We're still
on the air,

still on the air,
they say

Errands

The old
to-and-fro

is newly cloaked
in purpose.

There's a jumble
of hair and teeth

under the bedclothes
in the forest.

"The better to eat you with,"
it says

and nibbles us
until we laugh.

———

An ax-man
comes to help.

———

"To, To,"
birds cheep

to greet
whatever has come up.

"To, To"

Exact

Quick, before you die,
describe

the exact shade
of this hotel carpet.

What is the meaning
of the irregular, yellow

spheres, some
hollow,

gathered in patches
on this bedspread?

If you love me,
worship

the objects
I have caused

to represent me
in my absence.

—

Over and over
tiers

of houses spill
pleasantly

down that hillside.
It

might be possible
to count occurrences.

Money Talks

1

Money is talking
to itself again

in this season's
bondage
and safari look,

its closeout camouflage.

Hit the refresh button
and this is what you get,

money pretending
that its hands are tied.

2

On a billboard by the 880,

money admonishes,
"Shut up and play."

Long Green

Such naked spines
and vertebrae —

convincing parallels —

upright, separated

by a few inches
of clay.

Such earnest, green
gentlemen,

such stalwarts
jouncing

in the intermittent
wind.

—

"Idea laundering

exists primarily

to produce a state

of equilibrium."

All night
the sea coughs up

green strands,

cold boluses

and swallows them
back in

Number

1

The stirring
presence
here again,

the fresh
limpidity,

the green
dangle

which we
have always half
forgotten

or mis-
remembered as
our own.

2

To vibrate in place
for emphasis,

to trill.

3

The assumption, one
of going on,

budding off
into what

will be multiple.

4

What are later called
"functions,"

mirrored,

made into a
routine,

dazzlingly amplified
at first,

then merely
doubled,

surveilled.

FROM *Just Saying*

Scripture

Your violins pursue
the downhill course
of streams,

even to their wild
curls and cowlicks.

To repeat
is not to catch.

—

Consider the hummingbirds,
how they're gussied up

and monomaniacal
as the worst (or best)
of you.

Consider the bright,
streamlined emergency
they manifest.

—

My leaves form bells,
topknots,
small cups of sex,

overweening, unstoppered.

Not one of you
with all your practice

is so extravagantly
coiffed.

Instead

1

To each his own
severance package.

The Inca
hacked large stones
into the shapes of
nearby peaks.

2

The eerie thing
is that ghosts don't exist.

Rows
of clear droplets
hang from stripped twigs

instead.

3

Pain brings attention
to herself.

Spine on Fire!
Trail Blazer!

(Thinks she's hot.)

Out here
slim trunks bend
every which

Dress Up

To be "dressed"
is to emit
"virtual particles."

—

The spirit of "renormalization" is that

an electron
all by itself

can have infinite
mass and charge,

but, when it's "dressed" . . .

—

A toddler stares at us
till we look up.

"Flirtatious," we call it.

She waits
until we get the joke

about being here,
being there.

Accounts

FOR BRIAN KEATING

Light was on its way
from nothing
to nowhere.

Light was all business

    Light was full speed

when it got interrupted.

Interrupted by what?

When it got tangled up
and broke
into opposite

    broke into brand-new things.

What kinds of things?

Drinking Cup

    "Thinking of you!
        Convenience Valet"

How could speed take shape?

    —

Hush!
Do you want me to start over?

    —

The fading laser pulse

Information describing the fading laser pulse

is stored

is encoded

in the spin states
of atoms.

God
is balancing his checkbook

God is encrypting his account.

This is taking forever!

Ghosted

Long, loose,
spindly, green
stalks with their few
leaves, bug-eaten
tatters
on which
a black monarch
sits, folding
and unfolding
its wings.

2

A friend's funeral has broken up—

or was that the last dream?

Now I'm struggling
between monuments,

looking for Chuck.

It's getting dark
and I'm pissed off

because he won't answer his cell.

3

On the wall in a coffee bar,
a model's arms
and stern, pretty face
frame a window

(where her chest should be)

and a clear sky beyond

Spent

Suffer as in allow.

List as in want.

Listless as in transcending
desire, or not rising
to greet it.

To list
is to lean,
dangerously,
to one side.

Have you forgotten?

Spent
as in exhausted.

Haunts

I

Rock eaten
to familiar shapes—

heads cocked
on jagged spines.

How many
orange, pink, white
rock pinnacles
are visible from here?

Grandeur
is that number

plus distance,

as if "again"
could be made manifest.

"Nature" was a 19th-century fad,
cousin to eugenics.

In the 21st century,
America's soft core's
undead.

—

On how many bookstore shelves,
lovely, fanged teenagers,
red-eyed, smeared with blood.

The Look

The boxer crab
attaches a sea anemone
to each claw,
waves.

—

You, small flower-bearing stick,
what is your true name?

—

Spooked and spooked again.
It's cute

when the intricately patterned
black and yellow fish

twitches
and shoots off

in a new direction.

—

From birth,
you've been moving

your eyes
back and forth,

looking
to be hailed.

My Apocalypse

A woman writes to ask
how far along I am
with my apocalypse.

What will you give me
if I tell?

An origami fish
made from a dollar bill.

After the apocalypse,
we will all be in a band.

We will understand each other
perfectly.

—

"It's alright" and

"It doesn't matter."

Let "it" stand
for nothing.

—

A weathered, fleshy bicyclist
wearing bunny ears
and a tie-dyed shirt
says "Zoom"
as she coasts past

Arrivals

Sign in the airport:
It's not how much
Cloud,
but what kind.

———

Welcome.

"We don't play requests,
but we don't play bagpipes
either. We figure
that's fair."

That's the bad-boy
sass
of globalization

kick-starting you
on Clear Channel

where even the spin
gets spun.

———

Here's one:

The devil is a blowsy,
failed executive

who fires burn-outs,
star after star.

—

Every known object
rotates

as if:

       b. keeping busy
       c. stunned

Transactions

1

What do we like best
about ourselves?

Our inability
to be content.

We might see this
restlessness

as a chip
not yet cashed in.

2

You appear
because you're lonely

maybe.
You would not say that.

You come to tell me
you're saving money
by cooking for yourself.

You've figured out
what units you'll need

to exchange for units
if you intend

I know I mustn't
interrupt.

3

Hectic and flexible,

flames

are ideal

new bodies for us!

Scale

1

In my youth, I craved the small picture,

the autistic strung-out
hearts of ivy, star jasmine,

the "on and on"
without budging.

I liked Russian icons,

circles
within circles in

the virgin's halo,
the way her cloak

matched the sky which
was not the sky at all.

2

Now I see
that the outsized "personalities"

of our day,
the Brad and Angies,

have the blurred, grainy texture
indicative of stretching.

We get a faint ping
back
when we focus on these objects.

3

"An electron
is an excitation

in an electron field,"

a permanent tizzy
in the presence of

what?

Like thought
it creates the ground
it covers,

like thought,
it can't stop

And

1

Tense and *tenuous*
grow from the same root

as does *tender*
in its several guises:

the sour grass flower;
the yellow moth.

2

I would not confuse
the bogus
with the spurious.

The bogus
is a sore thumb,

while the spurious
pours forth

as fish and circuses.

Treatment

The relationship between a handsome young broker
and a lovely young curator
is in trouble.
Before they can marry, he must
come to tolerate,
then feel guarded affection for
a good-natured buffoon
who populates dioramas
with stuffed mouse couples in period dress,
then for an assortment of others,
some less likeable,
who also take passionate interest
in an activity that generates no profit.

Experts

1

I met a genius.
He's an expert on tourniquets.

No, turncoats.

No, tunicates.

He knows everything
there is to know
about sea squirts.

He knows what it's like

2

We coordinate our thrusts
by habit
to minimize distraction.

If an algorithm
has proved useful,

we believe in one
god.

We close our eyes
or stare

at a nonexistent
horizon

as if listening
for something vital,

faint,

some emerging
consensus
in the background chatter.

When certainty is high,
we grunt or yelp—

the agreed-upon signal.

One of us does.

Between Islands

1

If every eighth element
listed by atomic weight

is noxious,

is that proof of
intelligent design?

2

Here's your far-fetched plan,
glinting
in slanted light—

except "plan" is wrong.

Thought comes before
or after,

but you interpose
yourself

and that red hourglass
which you think nothing of.

3

Next to the thoroughfare,

between the shopping plaza
and the medical complex,

a man in a straw hat
leans
on a pink
pasteboard sign

with one
woman's shoe on it

and the word "Repair"

Luster

What flickers
with some delicacy

of feeling,

some hesitancy—
and then persists.

—

What circles. What darts.

—

Hunger

is like the inside
biting you.

"Like" is like
insomnia.

—

These green cherry tomatoes;
their false pregnancies,

staked. Lustrous.

—

"That's all I meant."

All I meant by
"witches."

Progress

The thickness of sleep,

the sense of swarm,
of nebulous propagation

from which we wake
by narrowing,

"sharpening,"

our focus.

———

The three weird sisters
are you,

babbling, in drag,

and what's so strange
about that?

They foresee your downfall,
but urge you on.

Where is there to go
but down?

You want to go,
don't you?

———

If we think dying
is like falling

asleep,
then we believe

wrongly, rightly
that it's a way

of sinking into
what happens,

joining the program
in progress

Bardos

I

Some say the soul
hangs from the ceiling
when the doctor pronounces
the body dead

and, afterwards, perhaps,
watches crises
in the lives of strangers,
bored

as we are here.

2

Let volume speak volumes.

One claims
he can recreate the sound
of a family argument
using bankrupt fishermen
and oil execs
to represent dead relatives.

3

One uses leathery
maroon tongues,
writhing,
laced up both sides
with gray shark-tooth spines.

4

I've been telling someone
(a cipher
emphatically)

how unfair it is
that so-and-so, a killer,
is angry

at his boyfriend/girlfriend
(unclear)

for being a "truck-stop whore"
when

Mother's Day

I wring the last
sweetness

from syllables
and consume it before you.

—

I make sense
like a scorpion

and the sun
will be smitten.

—

If I appear to address you
while quoting an old text,

I am indistinguishable
from nature

and therefore sublime.

—

If I reveal myself
mercilessly,

what will I not transcend?

—

Like God, I will leave

an arc
of implication

Meant

When the rat rests,
its brain

runs the maze again,
then runs it backwards,

and repeats.

This is early
music.

———

"Poetry wants
to make things mean

more than they mean,"
says someone,

as if we knew
how much things meant

and in what unit
of measure.

———

Some chords (crowds)
seem sad—

because uncertain?—

while others
appear quite resolved

FROM *Itself*

Chirality

If I didn't need
to do anything,
would I?

Would I oscillate
in two
or three dimensions?

Would I summon
a beholder

and change chirality
for "him?"

A massless particle
passes through the void
with no resistance.

Ask what it means
to pass through the void.

Ask how it differs
from not passing.

A Conceit

Local anchors list the ways
viewers might enjoy tomorrow.

One says, "Get some great . . . ," but
that seems like a stretch.

The other snickers, meaning,
"Where were you going with that?"

Like you thought

———

Like you could defend
vanity

in the sense of
idle conceit,

vacuous self-
absorption,

doing whatever
it takes to

whatever
because,

really.

———

As if to say,

"Conceit
is the vacuum energy."

Conclusion

A man is upset for many years
because he's heard
that information is destroyed
in a black hole.

Question: What does this man mean
by "information"?

The example given
is of a cry for help,

but this is accompanied
by the image of a toy space ship,
upended,

and is thus
not to be taken seriously.

The man recovers his peace of mind
when he ceases to believe
in passing through,

when he becomes convinced
that the lost information

is splattered
on the event

horizon.

2

The detective is the new mime.

She acts out understanding
the way a mime
climbs an invisible wall.

—

It's because our senses
are so poor that,

on CSI,
the investigators
stand stock-still,

boulders in a stream,

while a crowd
pours around them.

They pan
in slow motion, reminding us
of cameras,

then focus
with inhuman clarity

on the pattern of cracks
in a wall.

3

God's fractal
stammer

pleasures us
again.

Pitch

1

Beautiful,
the way the partita

progresses and retreats
(repeats?).

This node
virtually branching

on two "sides,"

without haste or
seeming intent,

almost reluctantly,
in fact,
almost "sending regrets."

2

Long-Term Technologies
has made these

fully nuanced,
self-reflexive stanzas —

sliver echoes —

"Silver Acres" —

widely available

to the shelter-in-place
public.

Eden

I

About can mean near
or nearly.

A book can be about something

or I can be about
to do a thing
and then refrain.

To refrain is to stop yourself.

A refrain
is a repeated phrase.

2

This table is an antique
from the early Machine Age.
The indented
circle within a circle
motif
which appears
at three-inch intervals
around the base
may be a nod
to craftsmanship
or may be a summary
dismissal of same.

It is *charming*
in its mute simplicity.

3

People will ask, "Why should we care about this unattractive character?"
despite the fact that turning yourself into an admirable character
has been considered gauche for as long as I can recall.

The word "transparent" is often affixed to such efforts
while the mystification surrounding the unflattering self-portrait
at least provides some cover.

Now someone will say, "You don't need cover
unless you're standing naked at a window
shouting, 'Look up here!'"

Sonnet 3

AFTER WM. SHAKESPEARE

Your dad told me to tell you
how good you look to him right now.
Check yourself out. (I'm sure you do.)
You're a very pretty boy.
But the thing is, that won't last.
Have you ever seen a pert old man?
An insouciant septuagenarian?
I thought not. They're invisible.
And you'll be invisible too!
What will your dad have
to look at then? Do you think growth
rebounds each year? Wrong!
It has to be outsourced. Sublet.
Get with the program.
Your dad will be watching.

Itself

I work it
until sweetness

rises
of itself,

then arcs across,
unfurling petals,

and is gone.

—

On television hundreds
of albino crabs
scuffle
over one steam vent.

—

I know you're dreaming
things I haven't dreamed,

wouldn't. But that's part
of your costume

like your extra
appendages.

Flo

In this spot for insurance,
a savvy young agent,
almost pretty,
says "Go Big Money!"
to a subordinate
tap-dancing
in a dollar-sign costume
in front of her confused/
bemused clients.

This agent, Flo,
who is above it all
but enthusiastic too
like the Dalai Lama,
has become/
is becoming
an American icon.

What I first saw
as tiny, novel
fireplaces scattered about
the living room floor,
I now see as the house gone
up in flames—
but this is wrong
because "first"
was part of "now"
from the very start.

Sponsor

We drove to the slough and walked briefly
along the uneven path.

There are plants here
you see nowhere else,
you said.

Pickle weed? Duck weed?

Branching pipettes.

———

Among twenty brown hills
the only moving thing
was the Coca-Cola truck.

Personhood

I

Imagine the recent dead
gathered in a parking lot
or lobby

wearing Victorian clothes
to distinguish themselves
from the passersby—

a flash mob .

They can't take themselves
or one another
seriously. It's hard

to hold on
to an idea

2

Clearly, each
orange parasol

of poppy,

having opened,
is one.

But effort is not
cumulative.

It figures
second
to second.

A self
is a lagging

indicator

Occurrence

Here's something about me.

I get up when sleep
becomes unbearable,
when dreams repeat themselves,
minor variations
on a randomly selected theme.

I go to bed
when consciousness becomes unbearable,
when the house repeats itself
and the television offers
to think for me.

Lay-offs accelerate
turn-around.

Aliens may try
to communicate with us
using black holes.

Here is what we know
about God.

If we are made in God's image,
God is impatient
without really knowing
what He wishes
would occur.

Headlong

As one
may be relieved
by the myriad
marigold faces
held aloft
beside the freeway—
their articulation—

and, too,
by the rush
of notes
following their own
likenesses
in these headlong
phrases

Relieved of what?
Relieved of what?

Believing

1

When did you first learn
that the bursts

of color and sound
were intended for you?

When did you unlearn this?

Believing yourself
to have a secret identity
can be a sign
of madness.

On the other hand,
the lack
of a secret identity
can lead to depression.

Many have found it useful
to lie down
as men
believing themselves
to be little girls

or as girls
believing themselves
to be mermaids
stranded
in their own bodies.

Head

1

You just feel wrong
so you convert

one neutron
to a proton,

emit beta radiation.

2

You try
not to squirm,

to cancel
yourself out,

still, in dreams
you narrate

each discharge
in the first person.

3

As if you were
banging your head

on every beach
in frustration

Control

We are learning to control our thoughts,
to set obtrusive thoughts aside.

It takes an American
to do really big things.

Often I have no thoughts to push against.

It's lonely in a song
about outer space.

When I don't have any thoughts,
I want one!

A close-up reveals
that she has chosen

a plastic soap dish
in the shape of a giant sea turtle.

Can a thought truly be mine
if I am not currently thinking it?

There are two sides
to any argument;

one arm
in each sleeve.

—

Maybe I am always meditating,
if by that you mean

searching for a perfect
stranger.

Rituals

1

In this now ancient ritual
a succession of young women

are saucy,

which is to say they name
common objects and relations

as if they had mastered them
but shouldn't.

Each receives false approbation.

2

As Xmas sells winter
to its prisoners.

As warmth
feels like love;

and love is warmth
only more capricious.

Fingers uncurl.

Organs expand
and rise

toward a surface
that must never

be broken.

The Eye

These brown piles
of stubble

hills

have failed.

They should be more

—

It should be difficult
but not impossible

to transmute
latitude

into a thought

a god could
hold.

—

Barred light:

dunes coming on
and on.

—

The eye, yes,
must move

to prevent
blank spots

from making themselves
known.

The New Zombie

1

I stare at a faint
spinning disc

in the black
endlessly

ready to pounce.

2

I actually say,

"I'm so sick
of zombies!"

3

Viral relics
in the genome?

Genes that switch
themselves off

and on,

unthinking
but coordinated?

4

Zombie surfeit.

Half-off zombie.

The best zombie
imitation.

Invisible zombie
hand

Expression

Give me your spurt
of verbs,

your welter
of pronouns

desiring to be spread.

Bulge-eyed, clear-
bodied brine-shrimp

bobbing to the surface.

I prefer
the hermit, trundling off

in someone else's
exoskeleton—

but we all
come down,

to self-love,
self-love which,

like a virus,

has no love
and has no self

Lounge Area

Stiff stilts of herself.

Silver bag of herself
with turquoise gilt
midriff.

(Shake it but
no more will fit.)

Red lipstick line
between the folds—

precise—

opposite baby's soft
gurgling.

Have you lost your
passes?

Greeks pictured the afterlife
as an insipid version
of the world they knew.

But they couldn't
see this.

Two women,
with red mesh crests
atop white hair,

enter the lounge area;

one laughs, "I feel
like we should
say something."

The Times

By "classical"
we mean the age

when the woods were haunted
by near misses,

not-quite girls
seen from the corner

of whose eye,
leaving branches

trembling
or strangely still.

2

The journals for sale here
no longer pretend

to be made from
dead animals;

now it's
strips of newsprint

and straw
that are retro.

3

It's the flimsiness
of the petals,

the way they're always
open-shut

though nobody
has seen them

move

ACKNOWLEDGMENTS

FOR NEW POEMS IN *Partly*

The author wants to thank the editors of the following journals in which the new poems in this collection appeared: The Academy of American Poets: *Poem-a-Day*, *The American Reader*, *The Awl*, *Barrel House*, *The Believer*, *The Boston Review*, *The Brooklyn Rail*, *The Economy*, *Golden Handcuffs*, *The Guggenheim Museum Catalogue: Story Lines*, *Lana Turner*, *Lanowich*, *The London Review of Books*, *Maura Magazine*, *The New Yorker*, *Poetry*, *The Poetry Foundation: Poem of the Day*, *The Volta*, *Zone*.

Many thanks to the editors of the anthology, *Privacy Policy*: Black Ocean Press, Boston, 2014

"Legacy": *London Review of Books*

"In Front": *Landowich*

"Exchange": *The Boston Review* and the anthology *Privacy Policy*

"Canary": *The Believer*

"Mistakes": *Poetry*

"If": *Lana Turner*

"Surplus": *Lana Turner*

"Assembly": *Lana Turner*

"Outburst": *Maura Magazine*

"Taking Place": *Poetry*

"Easily": *The Brooklyn Rail*

"Partly": *The Economy*

"Parallel Worlds Theory": *The American Reader*

"Word Problems": *The American Reader*

"Action Potential": *Zone*

"Torn": Barrelhouse

"Divisor": *Zone* and *Black Tongue Review*

"Life's Work": Poetry Foundation, Poem of the Day

"The Difficulty": *Poetry*

"The Ether": *Poetry*

"What We Can Say": *Golden Handcuffs*

"Voices": *Lana Turner*

"Overhead": *Zone*

"Altered Cage": *The American Reader*

"Transport": *The Volta*

"Sockets": *The Awl*

"Particular": *Maura Magazine*

"Lie": Poem-a-Day, Academy of American Poets

"Before": *The New Yorker*

"Followers": *Poetry*

"Approximate": *Privacy Policy*, an anthology

About the Author

Rae Armantrout has published thirteen books of poetry. Her books with Wesleyan University Press include *Veil* (2001), *Up to Speed* (2003), *Next Life* (2006), *Versed* (2009), *Money Shot* (2011), *Just Saying* (2013), and *Itself* (2015). She is professor emeritus in the literature department at University of California San Diego.

An online reader's companion is available at http://raearmantrout.site .wesleyan.edu